Oceans

Contents

Written by Anita Ganeri

Illustrated by Giulia Rivolta

Oceans

There are five oceans.
Can you spot them all
on this map?

Arctic Ocean
Indian Ocean
Southern Ocean

The Pacific Ocean

The Pacific is the biggest ocean.
It is the deepest ocean too.

This starfish lives on a coral reef in the Pacific.

The reef is under the water.

The Atlantic Ocean

This is the Atlantic Ocean.
Cod fish live in the Atlantic Ocean.
You might eat cod with chips!

This crab lives on the sand.
It digs a hole in the sand to live in.

The Indian Ocean

The Indian Ocean has warm water.
Lots of fish live in this ocean.
These are clownfish.

This fish is a lionfish.

The Southern Ocean

It is very cold in the Southern Ocean. Ice floats on top of the water.

This orca is jumping out of the ocean!

The Arctic Ocean

The Arctic is the smallest ocean.
It is very cold and
there is a lot of ice.

Polar bears live on the ice.
They have thick fur
to keep them warm.

Ocean Quiz

Can you tell which animals these are?

Index